IT'S TIME TO LEARN ABOUT CATERPILLARS

It's Time to Learn about Caterpillars

Walter the Educator

Silent King Books
A WhichHead Entertainment Imprint

Copyright © 2025 by Walter the Educator

All rights reserved. No part of this book may be reproduced in any manner whatsoever without written per- mission except in the case of brief quotations embodied in critical articles and reviews.

First Printing, 2024

Disclaimer

This book is a literary work; the story is not about specific persons, locations, situations, and/or circumstances unless mentioned in a historical context. Any resemblance to real persons, locations, situations, and/or circumstances is coincidental. This book is for entertainment and informational purposes only. The author and publisher offer this information without warranties expressed or implied. No matter the grounds, neither the author nor the publisher will be accountable for any losses, injuries, or other damages caused by the reader's use of this book. The use of this book acknowledges an understanding and acceptance of this disclaimer.

It's Time to Learn about Caterpillars is a collectible early learning book by Walter the Educator suitable for all ages belonging to Walter the Educator's Time to Eat Book Series. Collect more books at WaltertheEducator.com

USE THE EXTRA SPACE TO TAKE NOTES AND DOCUMENT YOUR MEMORIES

CATERPILLARS

A caterpillar, small and round,

It's Time to Learn about
Caterpillars

Crawls so slowly on the ground.

With tiny legs, it moves along,

Munching leaves all day long!

Its body's long and full of stripes,

Some have spots or other types.

Green or yellow, red or blue,

Each one wears a coat brand new!

It wiggles here, it wiggles there,

Climbing branches everywhere.

Eating leaves from trees so tall,

It grows and grows, so big, not small!

But one day, it starts to slow,

It finds a branch and stops to go.

Hanging still, it forms a shell,

A secret place to change so well!

It's Time to Learn about
Caterpillars

This shell is called a chrysalis,

Inside, it turns to something big!

No more crawling, no more chews,

A brand-new shape begins to choose.

It takes some days, it takes some nights,

Inside, it hides from all our sights.

Then one day, oh, what a treat!

The shell will crack, and out it peeks!

But wait! No legs to crawl around,

No more wiggles on the ground.

Instead, two wings begin to dry,

It flaps them fast and starts to fly!

The caterpillar's now all gone,

A butterfly has now been born!

It's Time to Learn about
Caterpillars

With colors bright and wings so wide,

It flutters high with so much pride.

It sips sweet nectar from the flowers,

Flying here and there for hours.

Floating through the air so free,

It spreads its wings for all to see!

So when you see a crawling friend,

Remember how its story ends.

A tiny bug that eats all day,

It's Time to Learn about
Caterpillars

Becomes a butterfly in a magical way!

ABOUT THE CREATOR

Walter the Educator is one of the pseudonyms for Walter Anderson. Formally educated in Chemistry, Business, and Education, he is an educator, an author, a diverse entrepreneur, and he is the son of a disabled war veteran. "Walter the Educator" shares his time between educating and creating. He holds interests and owns several creative projects that entertain, enlighten, enhance, and educate, hoping to inspire and motivate you. Follow, find new works, and stay up to date with Walter the Educator™

at WaltertheEducator.com

www.ingramcontent.com/pod-product-compliance
Lightning Source LLC
LaVergne TN
LVHW051919060526
838201LV00060B/4084